THE
ALGONQUIAN

by Rita and Mary D'Apice

Illustrated by Katherine Ace

ROURKE PUBLICATIONS, INC.

VERO BEACH, FLORIDA 32964

CONTENTS

© 1990 by Rourke Publications, Inc.

Library of Congress Cataloging-in-Publication Data

D'Apice, Rita, 1969—
  The Algonquian / by Rita and Mary D'Apice.
    p. cm. —(Native American people)
  Includes index.
  Summary: Discusses the history and way of life of those East Coast Indian tribes whose common language and culture related them, making a larger group known as Algonquian.
    1. Algonquian Indians—Juvenile literature. [DNLM: 1. Algonquian Indians.] I. D'Apice, Mary. II. Title. III. Series: D'Apice, Rita, 1969— Native American people.
  E99.A35D34 1990   973′.04973—dc20   90-8648
  ISBN 0-86625-388-2   CIP

INTRODUCTION

The first people arrived in America thousands of years ago. These pioneers were the first to discover America. Many years later, when Christopher Columbus arrived in America, he believed that he had reached the East Indies. Therefore, he gave the name of "Indian" to the natives that he found there. Today, the American Indians are called Native Americans, which is truly what they are.

As the population of these Native Americans increased, they began to fan out by following herds of animals or by moving elsewhere to seek fertile valleys and plains. Some crossed from west to east, finally settling in the woodlands along the east coast of what is now New England and in parts of New York and Canada. They became known as Woodland tribes. The land in this area had one common element—the forest. The Woodland Indians depended on the forests for food, shelter, clothing, and tools. There were many woodland tribes, but they are divided into two main groups based on their language groups: The Iroquois and the Algonquians.

Most present day Americans are used to seeing the word "Algonquin." However, Algonquin refers to a specific group from Canada. Scholars use the word "Algonquian" to refer to the entire Algonquian-speaking people.

Most Algonquian tribes lived in the area from Maine to Virginia, but the majority of them inhabited the woodlands of New England. It was the Algonquians who greeted the Pilgrims to the eastern shore of America. These Algonquian-speaking tribes included the Mahicans of New York state, the Mohegans and Pequots of Connecticut, the Narragansetts of Rhode Island, the Wampanoags of Massachusetts, the Penobscots and Abnaki of Maine, the Mantauk of Long Island, the Delaware of Delaware, and the Powhatan of Virginia. These tribes were the most powerful and influential, but they are not a complete list of Algonquian-speaking tribes.

The Algonquians were divided into several distinct tribes, but they shared a common heritage. Despite the lack of proximity of one tribe to another, they all spoke a common language, and, though it varied somewhat from one tribe to another, this unique form of communication distinguished the Algonquians from other tribes.

The Algonquians were culturally related as well. Despite small variations among tribes, their politics, religion, economics, society, and customs remained the same.

The Algonquian population was tiny compared to tribes such as the Navajo, Cheyenne, and Apache. By the time the Pilgrims arrived, there were only about 15,000 to 18,000 Native Americans in all of New England.

It was fortunate for the Pilgrims that the Algonquian tribes were friendly, kind, and generous. Without Algonquian help, the Pilgrims would not have survived. But as more and more white people settled in the woodlands, the Algonquians' way of life became endangered. The natives had reached out to help in the white people's time of need. They had taught the white people how to plant corn, hunt, and fish — how to survive in an unfamiliar land. But in return, the Algonquian tribes were treated poorly and eventually they were destroyed. This is their story.

THE ALGONQUIAN

WOODLAND TRIBES

ALGONKIN

MICMAC

MALECITE

ABNAKI

PENOBSCOT

MAHICAN

WAMPANOAG

NARRAGANSETT

PEQUOT

MOHEGAN

MANTAUK

DELAWARE

POWHATAN

Algonquian Language Spoken

WOODLAND TRIBES

A replica of the Mayflower II in which the Pilgrims crossed the Atlantic Ocean from Europe to America.

A Way of Life

LONG BEFORE Christopher Columbus discovered America, the Algonquian tribes inhabited the dense woodlands that stretched along the Atlantic coast. Living among tall birch, oak, and evergreen trees, these Native Americans had an abundance of game, fish, berries, and nuts available to them.

The Algonquian tribes were not nomadic, as were the Apaches. There was no need for the Algonquians to travel great distances in search of animal herds. Animals were plentiful in the woodlands. Tribes living in Maine and near the Canadian border, where snow covered the ground most of the year, hunted mostly deer, elk, and caribou. They depended on these animals for their clothes, food, and shelter. Tribes farther south were farmers as well as hunters and gatherers. They grew mostly corn, but squash, pumpkins, and beans were also staple crops.

Algonquian villages were small. About a hundred people lived and worked together in a village as one large family. Most villages stood beside a lake, a stream, or the seashore, with the homes clustered closely together for protection. Sometimes a village was stockaded, especially if it was the home of a *sachem*, an important chief.

The Algonquians shared everything — food and belongings. They were generous people who offered food and a place to sleep to anyone passing through the village. They worked alongside each other building canoes, preparing tools and weapons, planting vegetables, and building homes.

Algonquian Homes

Wigwam is the Algonquian word for "house." Most wigwams had dome-shaped tops, but they varied greatly in their sizes and shapes. A wigwam could be built round, oval, long, or short. Some were built to accommodate only ten people. Others could sleep up to ten families.

The men built the frame of the house out of saplings, tall, young tree trunks. The frame might consist of eight or ten saplings on each side, stuck in pairs firmly into the ground. The paired saplings were bent over until they met in the middle, forming an arch. Then they were tied with narrow strips of bark or root fibers. Crosswise supports were then tied securely into place.

The women did the rest of the work.

They covered the sides of the framework with woven mats or bark, and tied them to the inside of the framework. Light birch bark was used in summer and heavy elm or walnut bark in winter. The small doors — often one at each end — were also covered with mats or pieces of bark. In larger wigwams, each family had a fire for cooking. Small holes were left in the roof for smoke to escape.

The inside of the wigwam was cozy. Crude shelves, which held household items, food, colorfully embroidered mats, and woven baskets, hung from the walls. Benches covered with furs were for resting and sleeping. Most of the residents slept on the floor or on fur-covered platforms with their feet toward the fire. The fire burned in the center of the wigwam, providing warmth as well as a means for cooking.

Food to Eat

In the springtime, the squaws, or women, of the village moved to a nearby area to till the soil and plant crops and to gather nuts and berries. First they used a stick or a bone to break up the soil. Then they attached a large shell to a tree branch and used it as a hoe. Sometimes they used deer or moose antlers to loosen the soil. After the women had prepared the ground, they made small mounds of earth about three feet apart. Into each mound they dropped three corn kernels as well as bean, squash, and pumpkin seeds. Children helped their mothers to plant. It was also their job to shoo away the thousands of birds that were hungry for the seeds and the crops.

Corn was the staple of the Algonquian diet, so it was necessary that there be a good harvest. Fish was commonly used as fertilizer so that the same land could be used for planting year after year.

Squaws were also responsible for harvesting the crop. As corn became ripe, it was set out to dry. After it was dried, it was placed in tightly-woven baskets and stored underground.

The women also had to prepare the grain for eating. Yellow corn, called *yokeag*, was parched in hot ashes and pounded with stones into a fine powder. Squash and pumpkins were cut into strips and hung on racks to dry. Then they were stored in bags on the walls of the wigwams. As the tribe's gardeners, Algonquian squaws had limitless energy and deserve high praise. They raised the bulk of the crops and did so with rudimentary tools and little or no help from the men. Tobacco growing, however, was tended to by the men. It was grown for use in religious ceremonies, to be smoked for pleasure, and later for trade with the white people.

The Hunting Season

When the women finished their harvesting chores, the men began hunting. They had kept busy during the spring and summer sharpening stone blades and other tools, and making new bows, arrowheads, and canoes. The hunting season lasted from fall until springtime when fish and other seafood became plentiful, and it was time to plant crops once again.

A large selection of fresh meat always complemented the diet of corn and vegetables. Deer was the most plentiful meat, but the Algonquians also hunted bear, moose, and beaver. Wild turkey and ducks also were everywhere to be had. The occasional times when food was scarce, pigeons and crows were shot down and eaten.

The Algonquians used primitive hunting tools made out of stone, wood, antlers, animal bones, and shells. Bows were made from thin pieces of hickory, oak, beech, or rock maple branches. The wood was heated over a slow fire, polished, reheated, and bent into shape. Notches cut at each end of the bow held the bowstring. Made of animal skins or tendons, the bowstring was pulled tightly and securely into place from one end of the bow to the other.

The arrows were made from dry, seasoned wood. If made from young tree branches, they tended to wobble through the air, so great pains were taken to make sure the arrows were straight. Then, eagle, crow, or vulture feathers were tied to one end of the arrow. This kept the arrow on course. An arrowhead was tied to the other end with a strip of leather. The triangular-shaped arrowhead had a sharp point that easily penetrated an animal's body. Most hunters left the arrowheads in the animal's body after a kill, but they removed the arrow shaft and later refitted it with another arrowhead.

Game was hunted by various means. The men stalked, trapped, and snared their prey. Sometimes they hunted alone, but usually they banded together in groups of twelve to thirty men. The Algonquian hunter followed hoofprints and often surprised his prey while it was sleeping or feeding in the early dawn.

Many animals, such as deer, wolves, foxes, and wild cats, were caught in snares. The men attached a noose to a pegged-down sapling and left some acorns for bait. When the animal ate the acorns, the noose tightened around its leg. Then the sapling sprang up, dangling the animal in the air. When the hunters returned, they killed the animal and cut it down from the tree.

Women and children helped the hunters by checking traps each day. When a day of hunting was over, they helped carry the heavy packs of meat on their shoulders to the village.

Before the hunting began, Algonquians prayed to the spirits for protection, and thanked them when the hunting was over. Hunters never killed more than what they needed to survive; and every part of the animal was used. Meat was eaten, and clothes were made from the animals' fur and hides. Bones were used for tools, and tendons were made into cord. Animal guts and intestines became pouches that held dried foods, seeds, and personal treasures.

The Algonquian way of life was in many ways as primitive as that of Stone Age people. But the Algonquians' ingenuity and resourcefulness, as well as the plentiful availability of woodland game, helped the Algonquian tribes to survive.

Seasonal Changes

For the most part, Algonquian tribes lived in one designated location. However, it was common for them to shift their dwelling places within that territory depending on the time of year and the sources of food. In the summer, the Algonquians made their home at the seashore. There they enjoyed an abundant supply of codfish, mackerel, bass, haddock, and salmon. These fish were easily caught with nets, poles, and spears. Fish were so plentiful, however, that the Algonquians could sometimes scoop them up with their bare hands! Salmon were hunted at night, lured to the surface by burning torches, then speared or shot with a bow and arrow. Occasionally the men harpooned a whale from a large, sturdy dugout canoe. This huge mammal was cut up and given to neighbors as gifts.

While the men fished in canoes in the ocean's bays or sounds or on streams, the women and children hunted the shore for lobsters, crabs, clams, and other shellfish. Most of the seafood was baked in hot coals on the shore and eaten fresh. Some of it was dried and saved for the winter months.

In autumn, the tribe often moved again, this time to be near the forests and the animals they would hunt. After a month or so, the tribe would return to its winter village, where the people remained until summer. Each time a tribe moved, it left the framework of its wigwams behind, but took the mats and household belongings.

Ways to Travel

The Algonquians traveled mostly by foot. Narrow paths that connected neighboring villages wound through the woodlands, serving as links of communication between tribes. Some Algonquians were able to run up to a hundred miles in a single day. If an urgent message had to get through, a runner could carry the message to another village and return in the same day.

When families moved from their summer, fall, and winter homes, they traveled single file along these paths. Women and children carried household goods and followed behind the men, who carried bows and arrows to protect the families from wild animals.

Canoes were used to travel on water. Small river canoes could be handled by one or two people. Large lake canoes needed the efforts of eight or ten people. The Algonquians made two kinds of canoes — the dugout and the birchbark.

The dugout canoe carried up to thirty

10

people. It was the one used to move families, carry men to hunting sites, or fight in sea battles. To make a dugout canoe, the Algonquians cut down a large pine or chestnut tree. Then they stripped the bark from the trunk and charred one side of the log with a fire. Finally they hollowed out the log by chipping away at the burnt wood with axes, knives, shells, and scrapers made of bone.

Birchbark canoes were made mostly by Algonquian tribes who lived north of what is now Massachusetts. There, birch trees were plentiful for making the lightweight, sturdy and buoyant birchbark canoe. The birchbark canoe served as the swiftest way to travel, but making it was a longer and more complicated process than making a dugout canoe.

Although the amount of curvature in the bow and stern of the birchbark canoe varied from tribe to tribe, the basic construction was the same. First the birch bark was laid on the ground and covered with heavy stones to flatten it out. Then it was shaped on a frame of

poles. The sides were pulled up and secured to two main poles called *gunwales.* A series of stakes, arranged to flare slightly outward, was placed around the canoe and driven into the ground. Next the builders pulled the ends together and tied them securely with root fibers.

The canoe's lining was made from thin wooden strips laid across the length and width of the inside. To make the canoe waterproof, all the seams were glued with either spruce or pine gum and charcoal. It took about two weeks to make a birchbark canoe.

The white explorers who first sailed along the eastern coast in the 1500s were amazed to see the slender canoes skimming over the water. The style of these canoes was so perfect that it is still a model for present-day canoes.

Although most Algonquian travel was done by canoeing or walking, the Algonquians living in what is now Maine and most of Canada also used snowshoes and toboggans to get around.

Physical Appearance

The white people thought that all Native Americans looked alike. The fact is that the Algonquians varied as much in their physical features as white people. The men of the Algonquian tribes were generally tall, muscular, and strong. The women tended to be short. Algonquians' skin was bronze, but many had very light skin tones. The skin color also varied depending on the season and exposure to weather. Both Algonquian men and women often painted their bodies and faces. This paint, usually applied during religious ceremonies or in time of war, left stains that darkened their skin color.

Some Algonquians permanently tattooed themselves with colorful designs.

Men had little or no hair on their bodies. They plucked it out with clam-shell tweezers. Sometimes the hair on their heads hung down over their shoulders or was braided. Warriors shaved the hair on both sides of their head and let the center section grow high. Women wore their hair loose or braided over each shoulder. They combed their hair every day with a wooden or bone comb. The comb was usually covered with bear fat which gave the hair its shiny look. Sometimes they added feathers, colorful plant fibers, and a snakeskin headband for decoration.

Clothing

An Algonquian's clothing was simple but sturdy. In summer, the men wore only a deerskin loincloth. The women wore an apron or a long wraparound skirt made of the same material. Beautifully beaded soft-soled moccasins completed the outfit.

When the weather was colder, the Algonquians added skin shirts, fur robes, leggings, and feather cloaks decorated with porcupine quills and seashells over the loincloth. They also greased their bodies to ward off insects in the summer and to keep warm in winter.

Algonquian Children

Children were important members of any Algonquian tribe. They were allowed to roam freely about their village. Although chores came first, there was always time for play.

Babies learned to run almost as soon as they walked. Both boys and girls helped their mothers tend the crops. Boys helped make arrowheads. Their fathers taught them at an early age how to make hunting weapons and how to use them. Girls made wooden dolls and dressed them with deerskin.

Even the games the children played had a purpose: To teach them the skills they needed to survive as adults. Favorite pastimes were running races, swimming, and archery contests. Another was to play "follow the leader" around the village. A form of baseball was played with a long stick used as a bat and a pine cone for a ball! Dart games were very popular, too. The darts were made with bird feathers to help them soar high through the air.

When the children settled down, they listened to stories. These stories were told by older members of the tribe. Through the stories, the children learned not only about Algonquian heroes but also about their culture.

Religion

The Algonquians were religious people. They believed in one creator, a kindly great spirit that dwelled somewhere in the southwest. Good Algonquians believed that they would join the great spirit there when they died. The great spirit, who created everything good, was called Kautantowwit. An evil-minded spirit who created poisonous reptiles and plants was known as Hanegoategeh.

The great spirit showed itself through nature — the animals, birds, the earth, children, and even the sun and fire. The Algonquians worshiped and made sacri-

fices to both Kautantowwit and Hanegoategeh. Whey they needed sun and rain to grow their crops, they appealed to the spirits of the sun and rain. When children became sick, they prayed to the spirit that gives children strength.

Before a hunter killed an animal, he asked it to forgive him. The Algonquians believed that the animals they hunted did not die. Instead, their spirits returned to their villages. Their bones were treated with care and had to be kept away from dogs. An animal's skull was hung up, and prayers were said on its behalf. Bones of fish were thrown back into the water.

If a hunter arrived home with more than enough meat for his family, he would host a big feast in his wigwam. The people would gorge themselves with meat because the host did not want to offend the animals by wasting any meat. The doors of the wigwam were shut tightly, and no one could leave until all the food was eaten!

The great spirit expected the Algonquians to do good deeds. If there were a drought, flood, or disease, the Algonquians believed that they had done something to anger the great spirit.

One legend tells that after the great spirit made people, it became saddened. The great spirit realized that people would be aware of death, so he gave them tobacco which was supposed to make them feel good. Smoking tobacco became a part of the Algonquian religion and way of life.

Each tribe had a medicine man called a *powwow* or *shaman.* To become a powwow, a young Algonquian boy fasted, hoping to have a vision. If a vision appeared, it would look like a human. Once the youngster turned away, he would see an animal or a bird. The youngster was expected to collect a few hairs or feathers from this animal and keep this sacred token with him forever.

One of the powwow's jobs was to cure the sick. He did this by using plants and herbs and by making offerings of tobacco smoke to call upon the spirits. The tobacco smoke was used to drive away diseases. It was also used in almost every religious ceremony, whether it was a ceremony for planting, harvesting, hunting, or taking clay from the earth to make pottery. The tobacco that wasn't used for religious ceremonies was smoked or chewed for pleasure, or burned or buried.

A powwow also used a rawhide drum to call up the spirits. The drum was about the size of a washtub and was painted half red and half blue. A yellow stripe, which stood for the path of the sun, was painted around it. The drum was held off the ground by four decorated wooden stakes. Hand drums, water drums, and rattles made from birch bark and turtle shells were also used in religious ceremonies to call up the spirits.

Sometimes a powwow held a gathering, also called a powwow. During these powwows, the powwow dressed in special animal skins, painted his face, and drummed himself into a trance. People asked the powwow questions about the future or discussed tribal problems. Some danced and sang; others smoked a pipe. When the ceremony was over, the powwow came out of his trance and claimed not to remember anything that had happened.

Political Structure

Each Algonquian tribe was an independent nation, with its own land and its own leaders.

The tribe's chief was called a *sachem*. The sachems inherited their title by birth and were not elected. Most of the sachems were men, but occasionally a squaw sachem ruled over a tribe.

The sachem and a variety of subsachems, called *sagamores*, made up the tribe's council. Sagamores served as war captains and powwows. They held more power than the rest of the tribe's members.

The sachem was considered to be wise and able. His job was to take care of the tribe and to be a brave warrior and an expert hunter. Since there were no written laws among the Algonquians, the sachem had power over his tribe. He had the authority to make rules and enforce punishments. In order to act, however, all the council members had to agree with the sachem's wishes.

The people in the tribe supported the sachem by giving him a share of their game, fish, and crops. They also gave him gifts. Gift giving and receiving was an Algonquian custom. A man who gave many gifts was highly respected. The parents of a young brave always sent gifts to the parents of his bride-to-be, and her parents sent gifts in return. Likewise, parents of newborn children received gifts, and if a man killed another man, he was expected to give gifts to the dead man's relatives. Tribal members thought that the more gifts they gave to the sachem, the more favors they would receive in return. Most sachems were rich by the tribe's standards; they had to be, in order to influence their people.

Tribal property was kept in the hands of the sachem, who had the right to sell any part of the land. Some sachems were greedy and sold tribal land without the tribe's knowledge. But, more often than not, in an effort to keep peace among the tribal members, the sachem asked the tribe to agree to land sale treaties.

Wampum

Bead money, or *wampum*, was the most treasured gift among the Algonquians. White wampum was made from conch shells. The more valuable purple wampum came from the quahog clam shell. Wampum was difficult to make because the Algonquians had only stone tools with which to work. First, little beads were cut out of the shells, and holes bored in them. Then the beads were strung through narrow strips of deerskin. Belts, bracelets, and other ornaments were made from wampum.

At first only the sachems wore the beaded wampum. When the white people arrived, however, they brought steel tools that helped to create the wampum more easily, making it more available. The tribe's history was often designed into a wampum belt. Sometimes a sachem would offer a wampum belt to another tribe as a sign of peace. Wampum belts also were given as gifts at council meetings held between friendly groups. Whoever brought the most fancy wampum belt would get the most attention from the council members.

The Algonquians did not think of wampum as money. The idea of money was unfamiliar to them. But the white people realized how much the Algonquians valued wampum so they often bribed the Algonquians with it. They would give the Algonquians bushels of wampum in exchange for the heads of the white people's enemies.

Arrival of the White People

In 1492, an expedition led by Christopher Columbus reached the North American continent. Columbus was greeted by natives whom he named Indians. Columbus described these natives as truly generous people who would gladly hand over a possession to anyone who asked for it.

When Columbus returned to Spain, other explorers became excited by the tales he told. They, too, wanted to seek their fortunes in the New World. For more than a hundred years after that, European explorers sailed up and down the Atlantic coast. Few filled their pockets with jewels, but many realized that the greatest treasure was the vast, untamed land.

Almost all of the explorers who came after Columbus — people from Spain, England, France, and the Netherlands — encountered various Algonquian tribes.

The Native Americans guided the explorers through dense forests, sometimes carrying the strangers on their backs through rivers and swamps. They showed sailors where to find fresh water and offered them food. The natives even paddled out to sea in their dugout canoes to rescue sailors on sinking ships.

After a while, the explorers began taking advantage of the trusting Algonquians, many of whom were taken prisoner and trained to serve the white people. Others were forced to learn English or Spanish and to be interpreters with other tribes.

As more and more explorers returned home safely from America, Europeans gained more confidence in their chances of survival in the new land. Small groups of people began leaving their homelands in hope of starting a new life in America. The Pilgrims were one such group.

The Pilgrims survived a perilous journey across the ocean but they did not know the first thing about surviving in the New World. If the Algonquians had not helped them, the Pilgrims would never had made it through the first winter. Imagine America without Thanksgiving!

The Algonquians helped the Pilgrims even before they met face to face. The Pilgrims, needing to find a permanent location in which to live, sailed up and down the coast on the *Mayflower*, stopping occasionally to scout various areas. By this time, few of the Pilgrims were healthy. Many feared that they might die of starvation. At one stop, the Pilgrims found Algonquian baskets filled with corn. The baskets had been stored under mounds of sand near the shore. The Pilgrims took some of the grain on board to feed the hungry voyagers. Later, the Pilgrims paid back the tribe for the stolen corn.

For two months after settling, the Pilgrims lived without catching a glimpse of a native, but the natives were watching them. The Algonquians had heard stories of kidnapping and murder at the hands of the white people, so they stayed away until they felt it was safe. One day, a

messenger from the Wampanoag tribe came to the settlement. The young man, named Samoset, spoke to the Pilgrims in English. Samoset told the Pilgrims that he had learned English from sailors.

He offered to teach the Europeans about the land and his people. Samoset introduced the Pilgrims to the sachem of his tribe, Massasoit, a strong, serious-looking man. Massasoit wore an enormous necklace of polished bone and was surrounded by sixty warriors. A warrior named Squanto spoke English. Squanto knew the Pilgrims' language because he had been kidnapped and taken to England. He had stayed in England long enough to understand the customs and laws of the white people.

Massasoit and the leaders of Plymouth Colony were eager to make a peace agreement. Squanto helped to negotiate such a treaty between his tribe and the colonists. The meeting began with a great ceremony and an exchange of gifts as tokens of friendship. In the agreement, the Wampanoags promised not to attack or steal from the settlement, and the colonists agreed to protect Massasoit's people from hostile tribes. Both sides were true to their word until the death of Massasoit many years later.

Following the grand celebration, Squanto stayed behind at the colony to help the Pilgrims. He began by teaching the colonists how to catch fish, trap animals, and plant crops. Eventually, Squanto taught them how to grow tobacco, which later became a valuable export item. Squanto helped the Pilgrims until his death a few years later. Then, another of Massasoit's men, named Hobomok, became the Pilgrims' helpful guide and advisor.

Hobomok taught the Pilgrims more survival skills. He showed them how to tap maple trees to get sap to make maple syrup and maple sugar. Maple trees were new to the Europeans; the trees are unique to the northeastern section of the United States. Even today, people use age-old Algonquian methods to collect sap and make maple syrup and sugar.

Tensions Mount

If the Algonquians had wanted to rid their land of white settlers, they could have wiped out the newcomers during the first fragile years after their arrival. In the beginning, the Algonquian tribes didn't feel threatened by the white people because the natives didn't realize that the new arrivals were planning to stay. The Narragansett tribe thought that the Pilgrims had moved into the region only because they had run out of firewood in their own country! After a while, however, the white population grew significantly, making some tribes feel uncomfortable in their familiar surroundings. Some of these tribes made the decision to move away.

Even in the vast woodlands of the Northeast, relocating an entire tribe was not easy. Not all Algonquian tribes were friendly to each other, and peaceful tribes were reluctant to move into territories inhabited by hostile ones. Many of those who did move to hostile territory were captured and used as slaves.

Eventually, the Algonquians felt it was necessary to fight the white people to protect their land. The settlers were mostly farmers who were destroying prime Algonquian hunting grounds in order to plant crops. Knowing that their survival was at stake, the Algonquians took up arms and fought to protect their homes and families.

At first, Native Americans like the Narragansett tribe, welcomed Europeans. But, as more and more Europeans arrived and stayed, tribes grew uneasy. They were being forced out of their lands.

The Pequot War

The Pequot tribe of the Connecticut River Valley was the first tribe to react to the pressures of overcrowding. They felt themselves squeezed between the Dutch settlers, the English, and the neighboring Narragansett tribe, which was regarded as an enemy. Furthermore, the Pequots traded with the Dutch, which automatically made them an enemy of the English.

The Pequots had migrated to New England from the Hudson River area. Because of this, they were regarded as outsiders by other New England tribes. The smaller — and usually weaker — tribes resented the way the warring Pequots ferociously took over their lands and demanded tribute. The Pequot were living up to their name; the word *pequot* means "destroyers." When the Pequots decided to fight the colonists, most other tribes took sides against the Pequots. The hatred for these "destroyers" by not only other tribes but also by the colonists led to the Pequot tribe's eventual destruction.

Two separate incidents led up to the Pequot War. Two coastal traders, John Stone and John Oldham, apparently were murdered by Pequot tribesmen —

Stone in 1633 and Oldham in 1636. The colonists wanted revenge.

According to one story, John Stone had kidnapped a few Pequots to use as guides and brought them on board his ship. When he and his fellow sailors went ashore that night, they were murdered by Pequots who had witnessed the kidnapping. A shaky peace between the Pequots and the people of the Massachusetts Bay Colony followed, but the tensions could not survive the death of another trader, John Oldham.

Oldham landed on Block Island, off the coast of Rhode Island, after returning from a trading expedition into Pequot territory. Another trader, John Gallop, saw Oldham's ship swarming with natives. He suspected that the ship was being ransacked by Pequots, so he began firing at Oldham's ship. When all the native warriors disappeared below deck, an angry Gallop rammed his ship into Oldham's. Many of the natives leaped from the ship and drowned in the deep, dark Atlantic Ocean. Later, Oldham's body was found beneath a sail. It is questionable whether Pequots were justly accused of the crime. Narragansetts may have committed the crime since a few of them had been accompanying Oldham as guides. Perhaps, too, the Narragansetts were angry at Oldham for trading with the Pequots.

The Massachusetts Bay Colony, demanding payment in wampum from the Pequots, sent John Endicott to lead an attack on Block Island. Endicott's soldiers had orders to take Pequot children as hostages, but the Pequots stayed hidden on the tiny island. They huddled in the swamps while their cornfields and homes were burned to the ground. Still not satisfied, Endicott sailed down the coast looking for more Pequots. Before returning to Boston, he killed a Pequot and destroyed more wigwams near the Pequot River.

Now it was the Pequots' turn to seek revenge. Sassacus, their sachem, planned to lead the tribe into battle. First, Sassacus tried to establish an alliance with the Pequot's old enemies, the Narragansetts, but they were loyal to Roger Williams of the Providence plantation. Sassacus went ahead with his battle plans anyway, for, indeed, the Pequots were notoriously brave fighters who almost never lost in battle. Whatever the tribe lacked in sophisticated weapons, they made up for in courage and skill.

During the winter of 1636, Sassacus and his warriors descended on Fort Saybrook in the lower Connecticut River Valley. They taunted the colonists, burned hay fields and storage buildings, and killed cattle belonging to the settlement.

The following winter, Sassacus rode into the Wethersfield settlement, bought rifles from local trappers, and severely damaged property there. It wasn't long before the colonists gathered forces and planned to retaliate.

The colonists, being highly organized, had the advantage over the Pequots. Captain John Mason, an experienced fighter, led the troops. Almost half the male population in Hartford, Wethersfield, and nearby Windsor came out to fight. The Mohegans, Narragansetts, and Niantics, eager to see their longtime enemy humbled, joined the colonists as allies.

Captain Mason planned to sneak up on the Pequots and catch them off guard. Two hours before dawn, on May 25, 1637, his troops surprised the sleeping Pequots. Most were killed in their beds. Even women and children were slaughtered. The bravest Pequots held off the colonists for a while, but when the colonists set the wigwams on fire, the Pequots had no chance. Many died in the fire. Those who escaped were massacred by Narragansetts and Mohegans who had been waiting in the surrounding countryside.

It is estimated that at least 600 Pequots were murdered that day. John Mason was recognized by the white people as having saved the settlements from ruin. A monument to him stands on the site of a Pequot fort in West Mystic, Connecticut.

John Mason Monument.

(Photo courtesy of Mystic Seaport Museum)

Death of the Pequot Nation

The war didn't end after the May bloodbath. The colonists, thinking that the Pequots were messengers of the devil, believed it was their responsibility to finish them off. The remaining Pequots knew that they couldn't win any more battles against the colonists, but they at least partly avenged the death of their tribe by killing the family of the Mohegan sachem, Uncus. Then they concentrated on surviving the best they could under their failing circumstances.

Sassacus led his people westward along the shore. In July 1637, he fled to a swamp in the town of Fairfield, where he hoped to make his final stand. Some peaceful tribes in the area saw the Pequots' flight. They thought that harm was about to come to all tribes, so other tribes followed the Pequots into the swamp. When the English arrived, they promised no harm would come to innocent people who gave up. They said that only those who had killed white people would be punished. Natives who had not participated in the Pequot War emerged from the swamp, but out of pride, the Pequot warriors did not surrender.

In a thick fog, the Pequots fought to the end. When he battle was over, most of their warriors were dead. Only 180 were taken prisoner. A few, including Sassacus, broke loose and ran into Mohawk territory, but they hardly had time to catch their breath before the Mohawks beheaded them.

The Mohawks sent the Pequots' scalps to the white soldiers to prove that the Mohawks were enemies of the Pequots. But those who survived the massacre could not be called lucky. Many were sold by the white people into slavery in Bermuda or given as slaves to the Mohegans, Narragansetts, and Niantics as a reward for their helping the whites.

The colonists, hoping that the name of the Pequots would die out along with the people, tried to abolish Pequot place names. Today, however, despite that early ruling, the name of this once-great tribe is found on libraries, streets, schools, rivers, and hotels in the very towns in which they were massacred. In the same town where the Pequots sustained their greatest losses, there is an epitaph to the whole tribe. On one of the major roads through town, a monument marking the swamp fight reads, "Here on a July day in 1637, a Pequot nation died."

THE
GREAT SWAMP FIGHT
HERE ENDED
THE PEQUOT WAR
JULY 13, 1637

(Photo courtesy of Rita D'Apice)

24

The White People's Power

After the Pequot tribe was massacred, other Algonquian tribes had difficulties with the white people. They saw their hunting grounds shrink as the growing population of settlers pushed deeper and deeper into the heartland. Algonquian tribes were forced to hunt in territory inhabited by hostile Iroquois. And, although it was unintentional, white people's diseases, such as smallpox, killed off a large number of Native Americans.

The Algonquians were angry about the disrespectful and humiliating way in which they were treated by the white people. Instead of accepting the Algonquians as they were, the colonists tried to change them.

Missionaries tried to convert them to Christianity. Those few who did convert were looked upon with disfavor by other Algonquians. These "Praying Indians," as they were called, caused serious tension within the tribes.

Most of the Algonquians rejected the Christian God, and even accused the white people of not understanding how to worship. The white people, on the other hand, accused the Algonquians of being savages. The Algonquians, in turn, believed that the white people's greed was evidence of a greater savagery.

The Algonquians were suspicious of the missionaries' motives for wanting to convert them. They feared that the attempts at conversion were just another way for the settlers to use their power over the Algonquians and to trick them into submission.

The white people had the power to take the Algonquians' land. Sometimes the colonists stole the Algonquians' land outright. Other times they acquired it through deliberately misleading treaties. It has been argued that the Algonquians never fully understood the treaties they were signing. They misinterpreted what the colonists meant when they offered to "buy" land. When tribal leaders signed a deed, they thought that they were agreeing to share the land with the colonists, not to give up all their rights to use it.

(Photo courtesy of Plimoth Plantation)

Because of the white people's presence, the Algonquians' traditions and culture were being watered down. The Algonquians were accustomed to sharing all earthly goods, but the white people introduced complete ownership of material possessions. English traders also made the Algonquians dependent on European goods that the natives could not really afford. To pay their debts, many Algonquians left their tribes to find work in colonial villages. The Algonquians resented this dependence they came to have on the white people.

The Algonquians further resented having to be subject to English law. They found it unjust to have their crimes judged in colonial courts. They were no longer free to monitor the actions of their own people and to administer justice according to their own laws.

King Philip's War

A young Wampanoag warrior named Metacomet inspired his tribe to fight for their rights against the colonists. His father, Massasoit, had been the sachem who had helped save the original Pilgrim settlers. Metacomet himself was full of pride, energy, and bravery. The colonists called him King Philip. King Philip was outraged at the way his people were being treated. To make matters worse, he was bitter because he believed that his older brother had been poisoned by the white people.

When Metacomet came to power, he was harassed by Plymouth Colony officials who sensed the rising tensions of the Native Americans. The colonists hoped to intimidate Metacomet and his people, so that the Algonquians would be reluctant to stir up trouble.

In the beginning, King Philip signed treaties and turned over Wampanoag firearms at the colonists' request. He seemed to be complying with the white people's terms, but secretly he was working to establish an alliance of Algonquian tribes. Despite the lack of sophisticated weapons, Metacomet knew that the Algonquians could overwhelm the still-small population of colonists, but the tribes were unwilling to forget their grievances against each other. Metacomet had to continue his plans for war without help from the other tribes.

War finally broke out in Swansea, Massachusetts in June 1675. Colonists hanged three Wampanoags accused of killing a Christian native; warriors took revenge by killing cattle. When a colonist fired at one of the braves in his pasture, Wampanoag warriors poured into area settlements, killing settlers and setting fire to buildings.

Seeing that the Wampanoags had a chance at victory, Nipmucs and Narra-

gansetts joined in to share the spoils. Other tribes heard about the war and traveled from Maine to help. From the Atlantic Ocean to the Connecticut River, the Algonquian tribes left a trail of destruction. At least fifty-two of the ninety white settlements in New England suffered attack — twelve were destroyed completely.

The New England Confederation of Massachusetts called out several armies to hold back the siege. The largest battles were fought in Pocasset swamp and along the north shores of the Connecticut River. One final battle, known as the Great Swamp Fight, ended the war. It occurred near Narragansett Bay on a cold day in December 1675 when several colonists tramped through the snow and overran the Narragansett stockade.

Metacomet's efforts seemed doomed. Although the Wampanoags had some allies, the Mohegans, Niantics, Sakonnets, and Massachusets [sic] served as spies and soldiers for the English and would not help their fellow Algonquians. The Iroquois did their part to destroy the weakening Wampanoags, too. Metacomet and his braves had been plotting their next move near Albany, New York when they were discovered by the Iroquois, who drove Metacomet's war party back into New England.

The war lingered on for eight months after the Great Swamp Fight. The last two battles took place in Deerfield and Bridgewater, Massachusetts in 1676. Metacomet was cut down at Bridgewater. All rebel bands were hunted down and murdered before a truce was signed. Metacomet's wife and son and hundreds of other Algonquians were sold as slaves. After King Philip's War, there was hardly a Wampanoag, Nipmuc, or Narragansett left. Sadly, Metacomet's defeat marked the last time any Algonquian tribe would find itself in a position of strength or power.

The Last Days of Tribal Life

The quality of Native American life declined rapidly through the 1700s. The Algonquians desperately wanted to return to the days before the Europeans arrived. The Mohegan tribe turned to political appeals. In 1789, a letter was drafted to the Connecticut Assembly at Harford. In it the Mohegans stated that their world had been turned upside down by the arrival of the white people. They wanted to return to the days when they lived in harmony with one another and did not have to fight among themselves for survival. To this day, there is no proof that any colonial officials ever even attempted to act on the Mohegan's urgent petition.

As a people, the Algonquians had difficulty holding on to their past. They had become outcasts in their homeland. Many of them continued to die from white people's diseases and alcoholism. Some left New England for Canada to join Connecticut troops fighting the French. Others fought with the colonists against the British during the American Revolution. But it was the defeat of King Philip that marked the end of tribal life for the Algonquians in New England and along the Atlantic coast.

Below: Mohegan or Pequot basket made around 1860.

Above: Yohicake woven bag made of hemp and dyed porcupine quills. Mohegan, circa 1650.

(Photos courtesy of Connecticut Historical Society)

Algonquians Today

Most Algonquians live and work in cities from Maine to Virginia. Their children attend public schools and often go on to college. Some Algonquians live on reservations, but the reservations are different from the ones that are run by the U.S. Government.

The U.S. Government reservations that exist for Native Americans in the central and western sections of the United States extend for many square miles and house many Native Americans. The Algonquian reservations are different: Each New England state supervises the reservations located in it. The reason for this is that there are so few Algonquians left to live on large U.S. Government reservations.

The tiniest Native American reservation in the country is in Trumbull, Connecticut. It is about the size of a city block. Chief Irving Piper and his wife live there and operate a corner market and gas station. Their son, Moonface Bear, is active in Native American rights movements.

A larger reservation is in Ledyard and North Stonington, Connecticut. The land is not marked off. Mostly elderly people live here. A few years ago, the Algonquians bought back some of their land from the state. Descendants of the Pequot and Mashantucket nations have since been operating large bingo games that are open to the public. The money earned from these games helps to support the reservation and museum, and to provide local Native Americans with a better way of life.

The largest New England reservation is located in Maine, where about 600 Penobscot Indians occupy one island on the Penobscot River. Fewer than 500 Passamaquoddy Indians live on two

Princess Red Wing holds a rattle made from a turtle shell.

other reservations in Maine. Children attend elementary school on the reservations, but they are sent to high schools off the reservation.

There are a few places where the white people can learn about the Algonquians of long ago. The Tomaquag Indian Memorial Museum is in Ashaway, Rhode Island. This museum, which features Algonquian utensils and baskets, was once run by Princess Redwing, whose ancestry is a mix of Narragansett and Wampanoag. Each year a green bean festival is held there. People can listen to Native American stories, learn Native American songs, and watch ceremonial dances.

A short distance from the Tomaquag Museum is a restaurant called the

Dovecrest. Owned and operated by a relative of Princess Redwing, it serves authentic Native American food daily. Beside the restaurant is a trading post and a museum. The museum houses, among other artifacts, an old peace pipe called a *calumet* and a large collection of arrowheads. An Algonquian village built to look like one from long ago stands near the museum.

Although the Algonquian tribes have made some gains in today's society, they are not satisfied with their treatment by the white people. They are speaking out for their rights. Tribes are banding together with other Native Americans. It is important to them that their culture not be destroyed or forgotten and that their children be educated. They want their language taught in reservation schools and they also want the history of their people to be taught in all public schools. Likewise, tribal council members are asking the local, state, and federal governments for better medical care; they want treaties between them and the United States to be honored; and they want land to be returned to them. Most of all, the Native Americans want more job opportunities and an end to discrimination.

The Algonquians gave Americans many things. Much of the American way of life is intertwined in one or more Native American cultures. Almost half the states, cities, rivers, and mountains in New England have Algonquian names. Three examples are Massachusetts, meaning "at the place of a great hill;" Connecticut, meaning "land on the long tidal river;" and Penobscot, meaning "at the falling rocks." Today we wear Algonquian moccasins, travel in Algonquian canoes, and have fun sliding on Algonquian toboggans. We eat Algonquian food such as corn, green beans, squash, pumpkin pie, and maple syrup. But most important, the Algonquian tribes were responsible for helping the Pilgrims to survive. Without their kindness and generosity, the Pilgrims would never have lived long enough to have been written about in history books. In fact the Pilgrims probably would have vanished from the earth, never to be heard from again. If that had happened, would there be a United States of America as we know it today?

Women at the Green Bean Thanksgiving Festival at the Tomaquag Indian Museum in Exeter, R.I.

Important Dates in Algonquian History

1492	Christopher Columbus discovers the Americas.
1500-1618	French, English, and Dutch adventurers explore the Atlantic coastal waters and shores.
1607	Jamestown Colony is established in Virginia among the Powhatan tribe.
1620	Pilgrims settle in Plymouth Colony, Massachusetts.
1622, 1632	Many Algonquians die in major epidemics from white people's diseases.
1636-1637	The Pequot War almost destroys one Algonquian nation.
1667	First politically designated reservation in the country is established in Ledyard, Connecticut.
1675	The Great Swamp Fight determines the fate of King Philip and the Wampanoag tribe.
1676	The death of King Philip marks an end to King Philip's War and to tribal life in New England.
1789	The Mohegan tribe presents a petition to the Connecticut Assembly asking for peace between the colonists and Native Americans.
1788	Connecticut and Massachusetts become states.
1790	Rhode Island becomes a state.
1820	Maine becomes a state.
1850s	Many Pequots leave the Northeast for Wisconsin to escape overcrowded land.
1853	State of Connecticut illegally sells reservation land to private individuals.
1924	Citizenship Act confers U.S. citizenship on Native Americans.
1966	American Indian Movement (AIM) is organized.
1978	Parcels of land near Providence, Rhode Island that were taken illegally from the Narragansett tribe are returned to them.
1979	Native Americans perform their rituals in front of the Statue of Chief Massasoit at Plymouth, Massachusetts on Thanksgiving Day to protest injustices to Native Americans.
1980	U.S. Government returns 12.5 million acres of land, taken illegally more than 150 years ago, to the Penobscot and Passamaquoddy tribes of Maine.
1983	Members of the Mashantucket and Pequot nations of eastern Connecticut begin purchasing 220 acres of land adjacent to their reservation from the people living there. This is done with a $900,000 government grant.
1986	Public bingo games operated by Mashantucket and Pequot Indians open in Ledyard, Connecticut.

INDEX